sundance™
LITTLE RED READERS

Colors

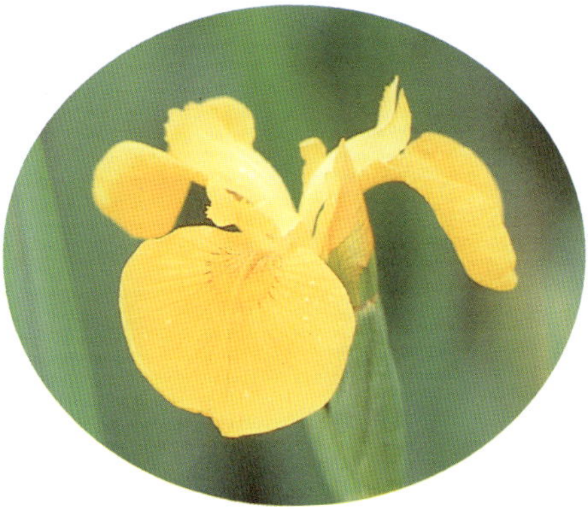

PETER SLOAN &
SHERYL SLOAN

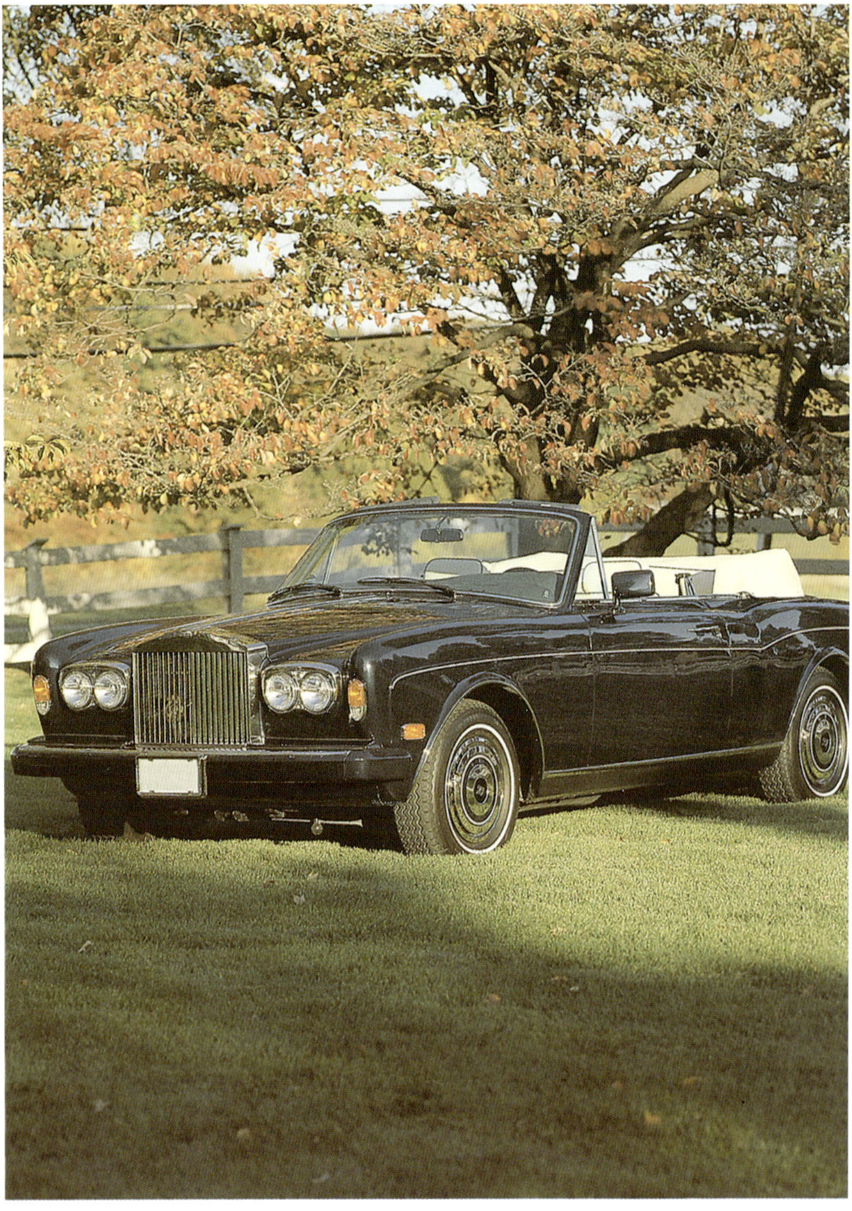

This car is black.

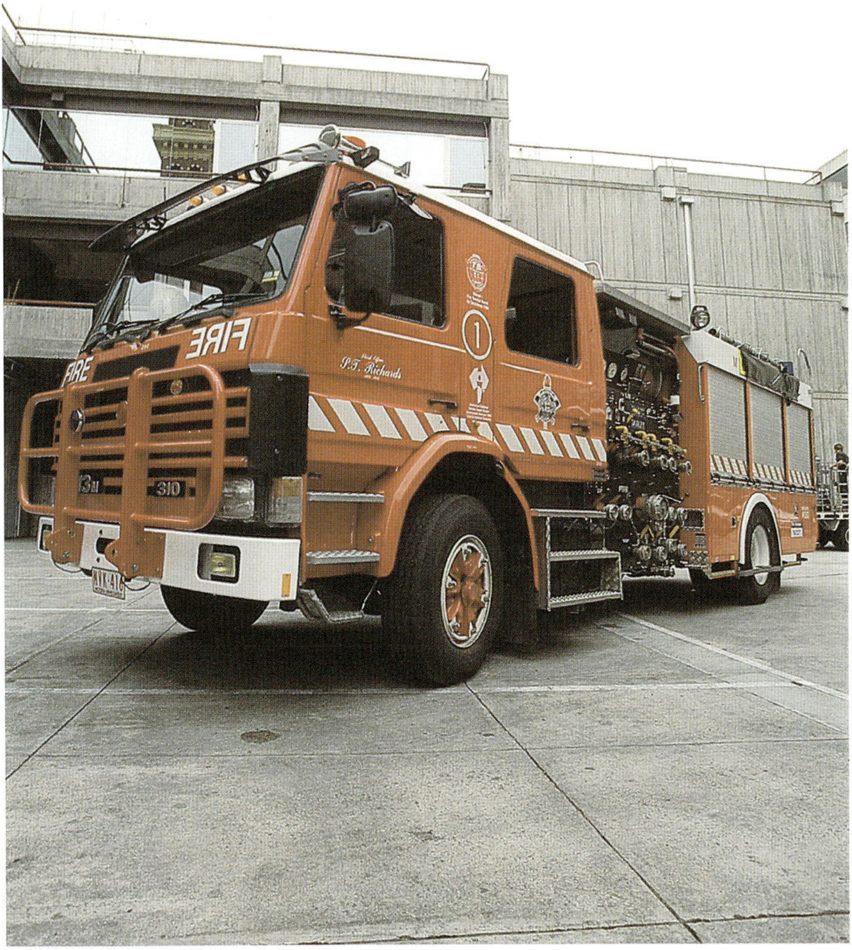

This fire engine is red.

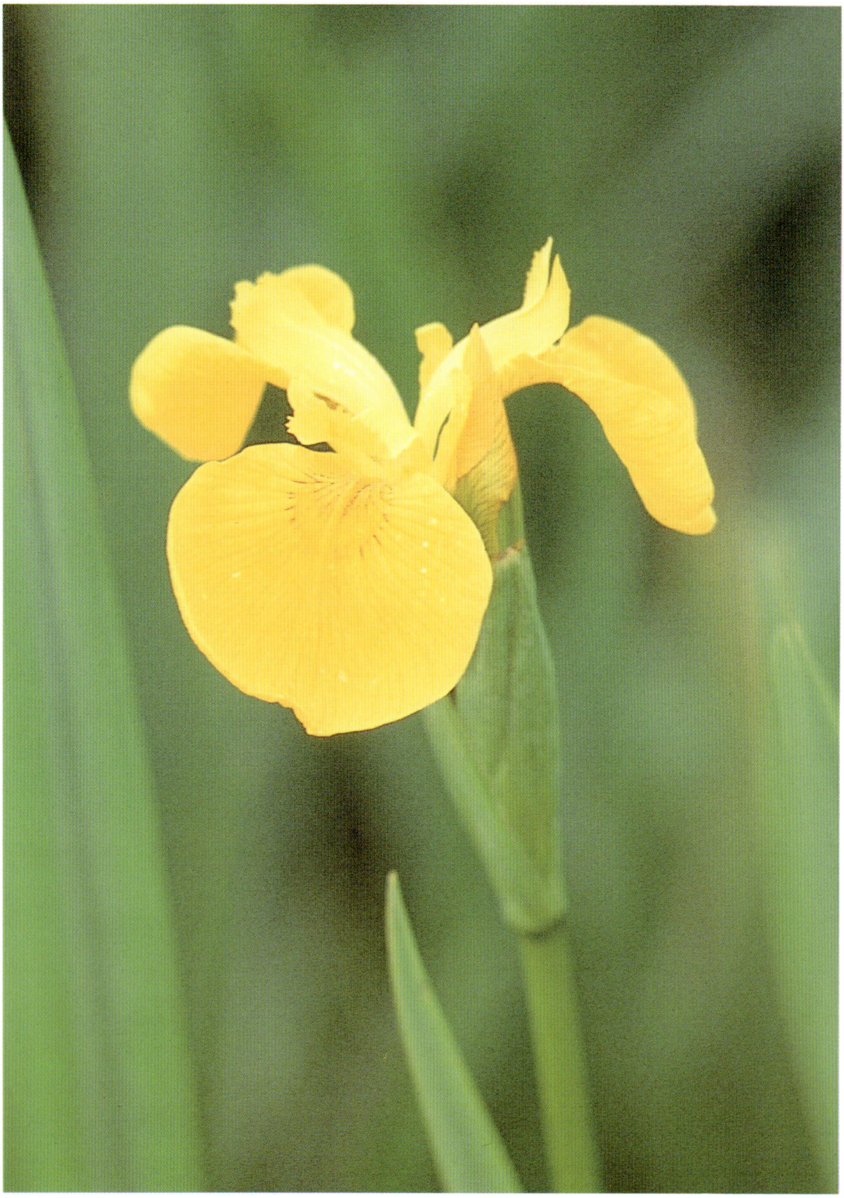

This flower is yellow.

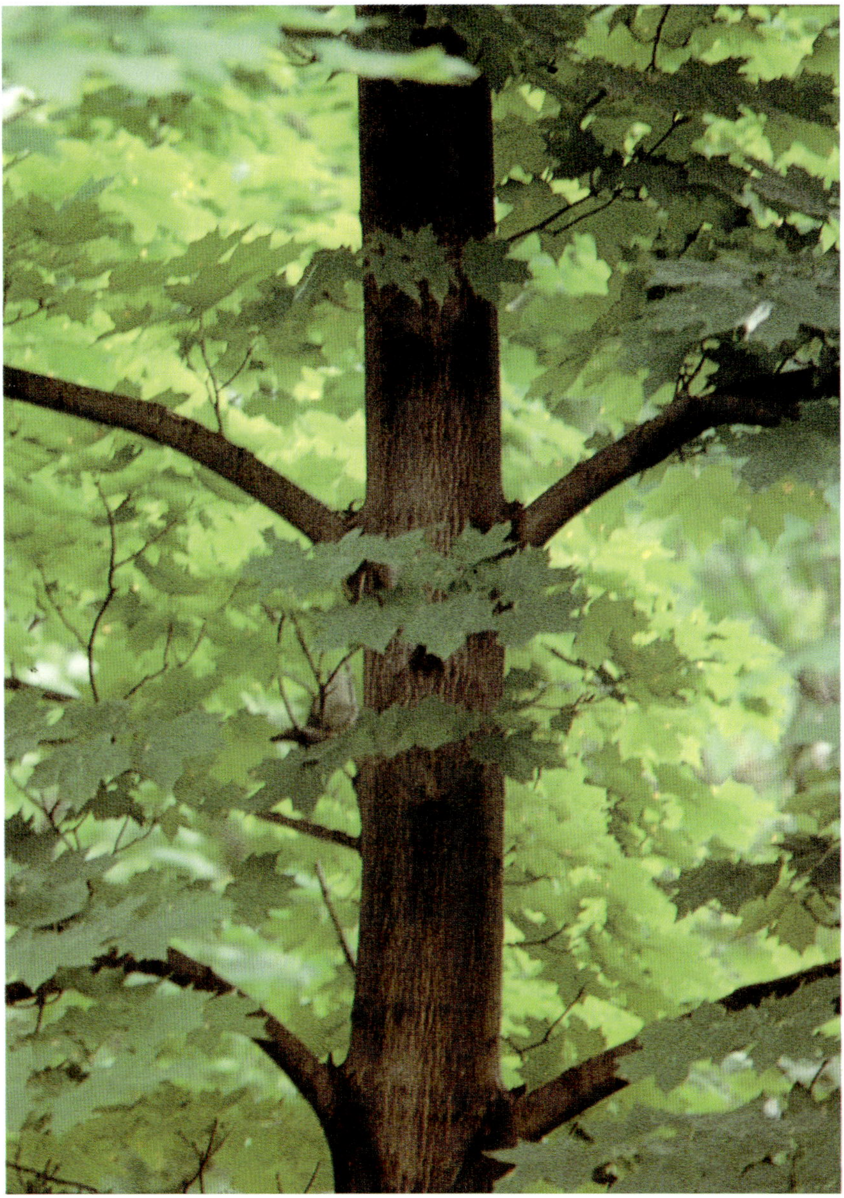

This tree is green.

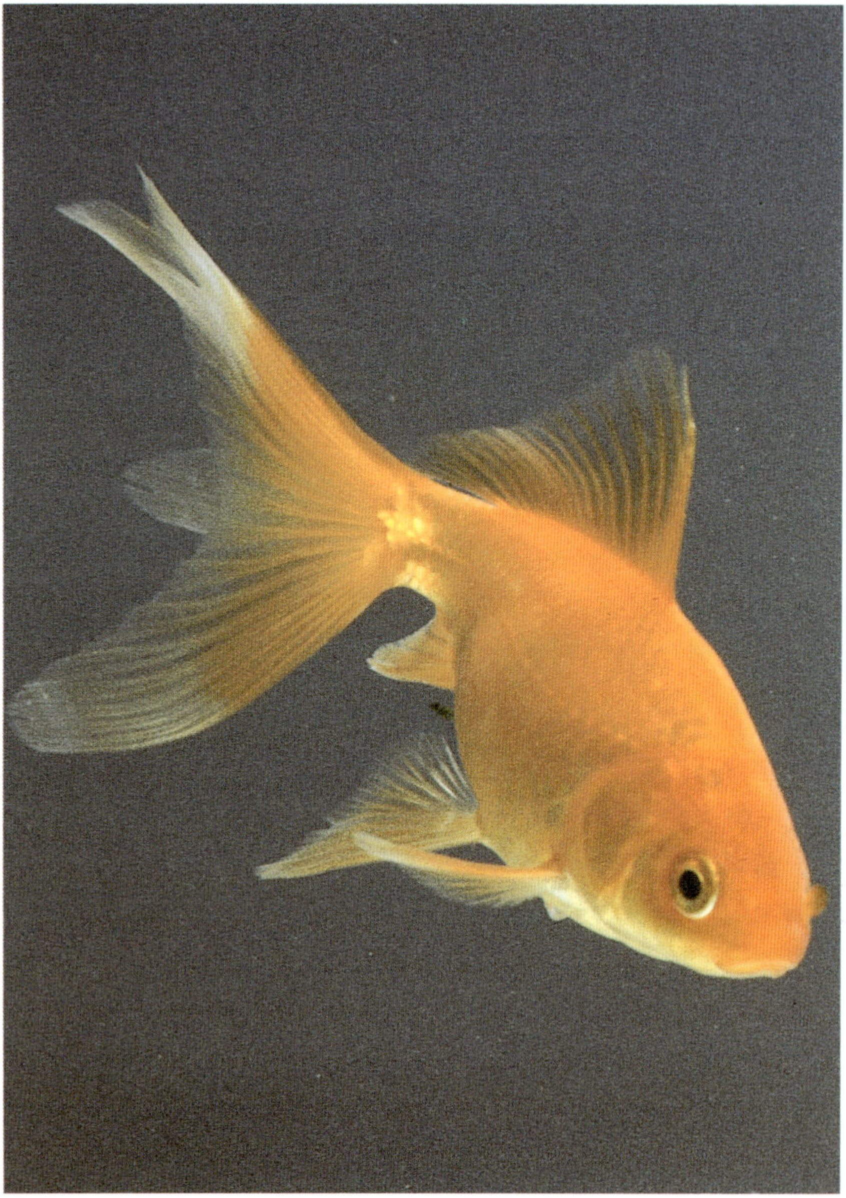

This fish is orange.

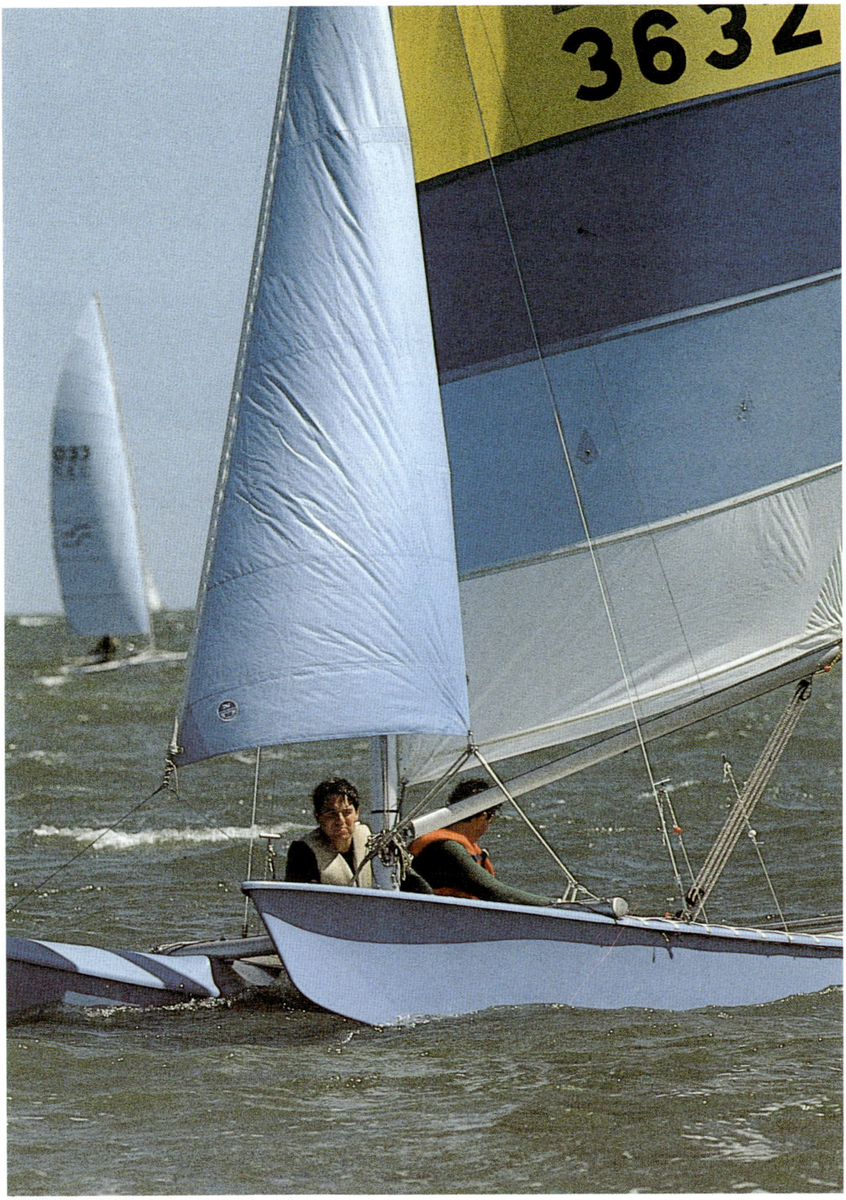

This boat is blue.

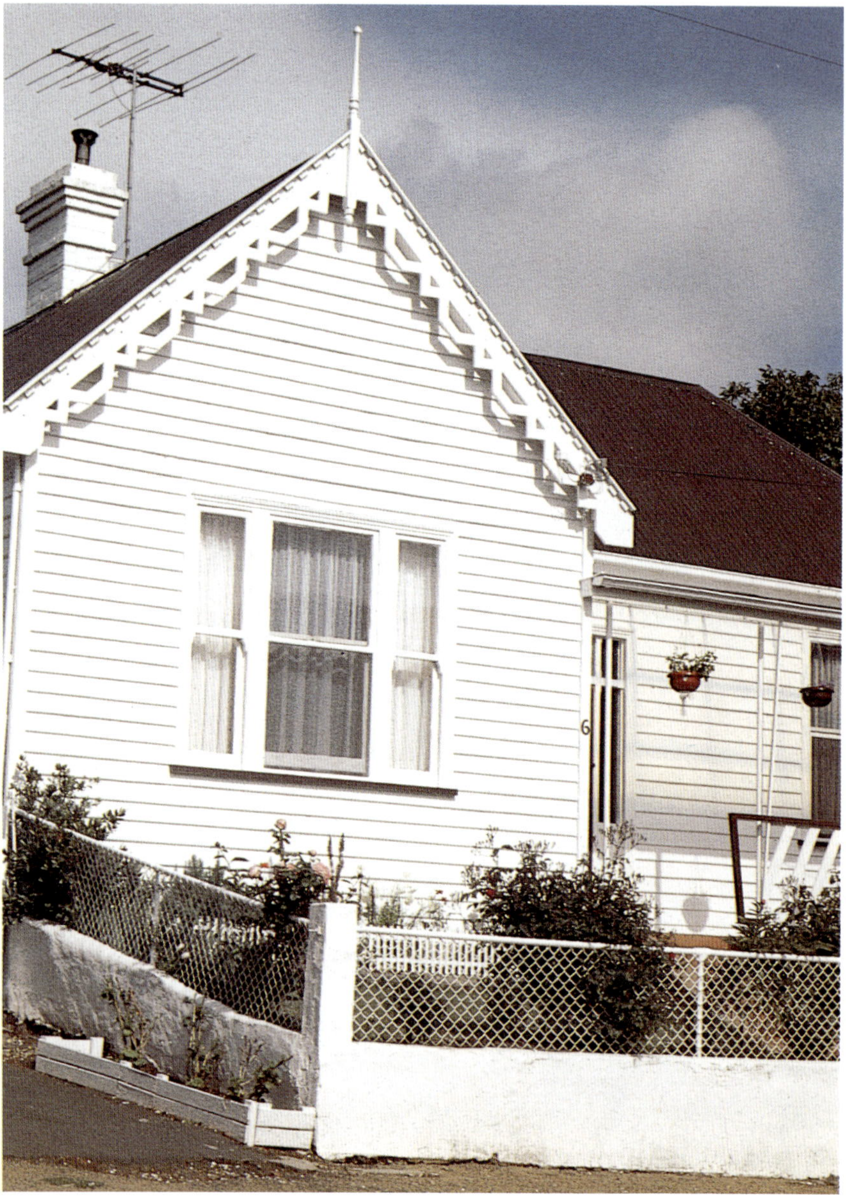

This house is white.